Grade
3
Ages 8–9

D1401694

Master Math at Home

Extra Challenges

Scan the QR code to help
your child's learning at home.

mastermathathome.com

How to use this book

Math — No Problem! created **Master Math at Home** to help children develop fluency in the subject and a rich understanding of core concepts.

Key features of the Master Math at Home books include:

- Carefully designed lessons that provide structure, but also allow flexibility in how they're used.

- Speech bubbles containing content designed to spark diverse conversations, with many discussion points that don't have obvious "right" or "wrong" answers.

- Rich illustrations that will guide children to a discussion of shapes and units of measurement, allowing them to make connections to the wider world around them.

- Exercises that allow a flexible approach and can be adapted to suit any child's cognitive or functional ability.

- Clearly laid-out pages that encourage children to practice a range of higher-order skills.

- A community of friendly and relatable characters who introduce each lesson and come along as your child progresses through the series.

You can see more guidance on how to use these books at **mastermathathome.com**.

We're excited to share all the ways you can learn math!

Math — No Problem!
mastermathathome.com
www.mathnoproblem.com
hello@mathnoproblem.com

First American Edition, 2022
Published in the United States by DK Publishing
1745 Broadway, 20th Floor, New York, NY 10019

22 23 24 25 26 10 9 8 7 6 5 4 3 2 1
002–327144–Nov/2022

This book was made with Forest Stewardship Council™ certified paper—one small step in DK's commitment to a sustainable future. For more information go to www.dk.com/our-green-pledge

A catalog record for this book is available from the Library of Congress.

ISBN: 978-0-7440-5198-8
Printed and bound in China

For the curious
www.dk.com

Acknowledgments

The publisher would like to thank the authors and consultants Andy Psarianos, Judy Hornigold, Adam Gifford, Dr. Wong Khoon Yoong, and Dr. Anne Hermanson.

The Castledown typeface has been used with permission from the Colophon Foundry.

Contents

	Page
Making and Comparing Numbers	4
Adding Using Mental Strategies	6
Subtracting Using Mental Strategies	8
Addition and Subtraction	10
Multiplying with Renaming	12
Dividing with Renaming	14
Multiplication and Division	16
Adding and Subtracting Fractions	18
Equivalent Fractions	20
Comparing Fractions	22
Sharing More Than 1	24
Measuring Time	26
Changing Years to Months	28
Capacity and Volume	30
Estimating Amounts of Money	32
Writing Amounts of Money	34
Calculating Change	36
Calculating Amounts of Money	38
Geometry: Perimeter	40
Measuring Area	42
Roman Numerals	44
Answers	46

Ruby   Elliott   Amira   Charles   Lulu   Sam   Oak   Holly   Ravi   Emma   Jacob   Hannah

Making and Comparing Numbers

Holly uses these digits to make 3-digit numbers.

What is the greatest 3-digit even number she can make?
What is the greatest 3-digit odd number she can make?
What is the greatest number she can make?

Example

Holly makes these 3-digit even numbers.
368, 386, 638, 836

836 has more hundreds than the other numbers.
The greatest 3-digit even number Holly can make is 836.

Holly makes these 3-digit odd numbers.
683, 863

863 has more hundreds than 683.
863 is the greatest 3-digit odd number Holly can make.

Compare 836 and 863.

836 and 863 have an equal
number of hundreds.
863 has more tens.
863 is the greatest number Holly can make.

Look at the hundreds.

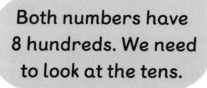

Both numbers have 8 hundreds. We need to look at the tens.

4

1 | 3 | | 7 | | 4 | | 8 | | 1 |

Use the digits above to make:

(a) the greatest 3-digit even number

(b) the smallest 3-digit even number

(c) the greatest 3-digit odd number

(d) the smallest 3-digit odd number

2 Put the numbers you made in order from smallest to greatest.

☐ , ☐ , ☐ , ☐

3 (a) Use the digits below to make all the possible 3-digit numbers.

| 9 | | 6 | | 3 |

(b) Put the numbers you made in order from greatest to smallest.

Adding Using Mental Strategies

Starter

Amira's dad needs to buy a new piano and an electric guitar for his band. The piano he likes costs $4999 and the electric guitar costs $1999.

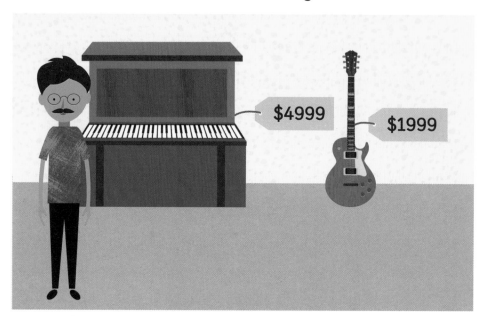

How much will Amira's dad pay if he buys the two musical instruments?

Example

We need to find the sum of 1999 and 4999 to get the total cost.

We can add them this way.

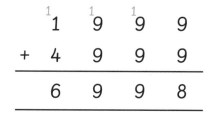

$$
\begin{array}{r}
\overset{1}{1}\ \overset{1}{9}\ \overset{1}{9}\ 9 \\
+\ 4\ 9\ 9\ 9 \\
\hline
6\ 9\ 9\ 8 \\
\hline
\end{array}
$$

There is an easier way. We can add 1 to 1999 and 1 to 4999.

$1999 + 1 = 2000$

$4999 + 1 = 5000$

I already know the sum.
$2000 + 5000 = 7000$

We must not forget to remove the 2 that we added to find the correct sum.
$7000 - 2 = 6998$

If Amira's dad buys the two musical instruments he will pay $6998.

Practice

Add using mental strategies.

1 (a) $2345 + 10 =$ ☐

(b) $100 + 587 =$ ☐

$2345 + 9 =$ ☐

$99 + 587 =$ ☐

(c) $3269 + 500 =$ ☐

(d) $4231 + 4000 =$ ☐

$3269 + 499 =$ ☐

$4231 + 3998 =$ ☐

2 (a) $999 + 2999 =$ ☐

(b) $999 + 3001 =$ ☐

(c) $5997 + 998 =$ ☐

(d) $3998 + 5998 =$ ☐

Subtracting Using Mental Strategies

Starter

Amira's dad cannot spend $6998 on musical instruments as it is too much money. The shopkeeper tells him that if he buys secondhand instruments, he will save $2999.

$4999

$1999

How much will Amira's dad pay if he buys the secondhand musical instruments?

Example

We can use this method to find the cost of the secondhand instruments. I know this method always works.

$$
\begin{array}{r}
\overset{5}{\cancel{6}}\;\overset{18}{\cancel{9}}\;\overset{18}{\cancel{9}}\;\overset{18}{\cancel{8}} \\
-\;2\;\;9\;\;9\;\;9 \\
\hline
3\;\;9\;\;9\;\;9 \\
\hline
\end{array}
$$

There is an easier way. We can add 1 to both numbers so we can easily subtract.

6998 + 1 = 6999

2999 + 1 = 3000

8

When we add the same amount to both numbers, the difference remains the same.

We can subtract 3000 from 6999 easily.
6999 – 3000 = 3999

We can also use a number line to help us find the difference.

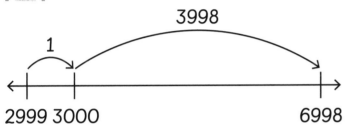

3998

1

2999 3000   6998

$3000 - 2999 = 1$
$6998 - 3000 = 3998$
$1 + 3998 = 3999$

Amira's dad will pay $3999 if he buys the second-hand musical instruments.

Practice

Subtract using mental strategies.

1   (a)   43 – 19 = ☐   (b)   101 – 99 = ☐

(c)   803 – 198 = ☐   (d)   1000 – 326 = ☐

(e)   5000 – 1674 = ☐   (f)   9008 – 99 = ☐

2   (a)   1001 – 999 = ☐   (b)   1001 – 199 = ☐

(c)   700 – 675 = ☐   (d)   1700 – 1575 = ☐

Addition and Subtraction

Starter

A garden center has 1285 tulip bulbs and 3634 daffodil bulbs. It sells 468 tulip bulbs and 1532 daffodil bulbs.
How many bulbs are left at the garden center altogether?

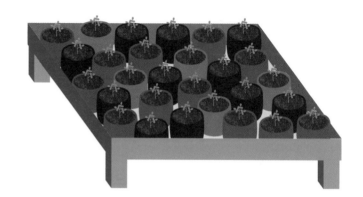

Example

We can add both types of bulbs together to find the total amount of bulbs they started with.

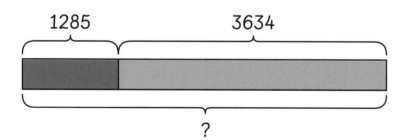

1285   3634

?

$$
\begin{array}{r}
1 \ \overset{1}{2} \ 8 \ 5 \\
+ \ 3 \ 6 \ 3 \ 4 \\
\hline
4 \ 9 \ 1 \ 9
\end{array}
$$

We can find the sum of the bulbs they sold by adding 468 to 1532.

The garden center started with 4919 bulbs altogether.

468 + 1532 can be added like this. The garden center sold 2000 bulbs in total.

468 + 32 = 500
500 + 1500 = 2000
468 + 1532 = 2000

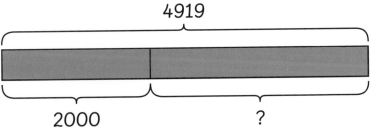

Now we can subtract the number of bulbs they sold from the number of bulbs they started with.

4919

2000   ?

4919 − 2000 = 2919

There are 2919 bulbs left at the garden center.

Practice

In one day, a baker bakes 396 white dinner rolls.
He bakes 129 more brown dinner rolls than white dinner rolls.

1 How many brown dinner rolls does he bake?

He bakes ⬚ brown dinner rolls.

2 How many dinner rolls does he bake altogether?

He bakes ⬚ dinner rolls altogether.

3 A supermarket buys half of the white dinner rolls and 500 brown dinner rolls. Altogether, how many dinner rolls are left over?

Altogether, ⬚ dinner rolls are left over.

Multiplying with Renaming

Starter

Each episode of Elliott's favorite show is 36 minutes long. In one month, Elliott watches 7 episodes.
How many minutes of the show does Elliott watch in one month?

Example

Method 1

```
   h   t   o
       3   6
 ×         7
 ─────────────
       4   2
   2   1   0
 ─────────────
   2   5   2
 ─────────────
```

Start by multiplying the ones and then multiply the tens.

Method 2

```
   h   t   o
      ⁴3   6
 ×         7
 ─────────────
   2   5   2
 ─────────────
```

42 ones = 4 tens + 2 ones

36 × 7 = 252

Elliott watches 252 minutes of the show in one month.

1 There are 7 classrooms in a school. There is 1 box of rulers in each classroom. Each box contains 42 rulers.
How many rulers are in the 7 classrooms altogether?

[ ] × [ ] = [ ]

There are [ ] rulers in the 7 classrooms altogether.

2 Emma, Ravi, and Ruby each buy some packs of stickers.
Each pack contains 24 stickers.
Emma buys 2 packs. Ravi buys twice as many packs as Emma buys.
Ruby buys 1 less pack than Ravi buys.
How many stickers do the children buy altogether?

[ ] × [ ] = [ ]

The children buy [ ] stickers altogether.

Dividing with Renaming

Starter

Seventy-eight children take part in a sports event. The children arrange themselves into teams of 6.
How many teams of 6 children can they make?

Example

Divide 78 by 6.

$$6 \overline{)\ \begin{array}{cc} 1 & 3 \\ 7 & {}_1 8 \end{array}}$$

78 = 60 + 18

1 ten + 8 ones = 18

We can make 10 groups of 6 from 60. This leaves 1 ten and 8 ones.

78 ÷ 6 = 13

Divide 18 by 6.
We can make 3 groups of 6.

They can make 13 teams of 6 children.

Practice

1 A teacher shares a bag of tennis balls equally between 5 children.
There are 70 tennis balls in the bag.
How many tennis balls does each child get?

☐ ÷ ☐ = ☐

Each child gets ☐ tennis balls.

2 Charles and Sam donate 52 books to the school fair.
They put all of their books into piles of 4.
How many piles of books do they make?

[ ] ÷ [ ] = [ ]

They make [ ] piles of books.

3 Ravi, Emma, and Holly each have 28 flower seeds.
They plant the seeds in the garden in rows of 6.
How many rows of seeds do the children plant altogether?

3 × 28 = [ ]

[ ] ÷ [ ] = [ ]

The children plant [ ] rows of seeds altogether.

Multiplication and Division

Starter

Charles, Elliott, and Hannah count their crayons. They have 95 crayons altogether. Charles has twice as many as Elliott has. Hannah has 5 less than Elliott has.
How many crayons does each of them have?

Example

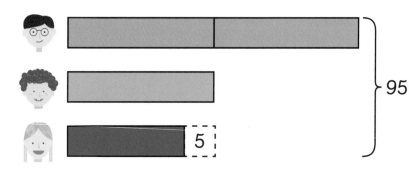

95

If I had 5 more crayons, I would have the same number of crayons as Elliott has.

100 ÷ 4 = 25

Charles has 50 crayons, Elliott has 25 crayons, and Hannah has 20 crayons.

Practice

1. Emma and Lulu have 48 books between them.
   Lulu has 12 more books than Emma has.
   How many books does Lulu have?

Lulu has [ ] books.

2 There are 3 buses taking 100 children to the theater.
Bus A takes three times as many children as Bus B takes.
Bus C takes 10 more children than Bus B takes.
How many children does each bus take?

Bus A takes

☐ children.

Bus B takes

☐ children.

Bus C takes

☐ children.

3 There are twice as many yellow crayons in a tray as brown crayons.
There are 3 times as many black crayons as brown crayons.
There are 56 yellow crayons.
How many crayons are there altogether?

There are ☐ crayons altogether.

Adding and Subtracting Fractions

Starter

A granola bar is cut into 6 equal pieces. Ruby takes 2 pieces. Sam takes 3 pieces. What fraction of the oat slice is left?

Example

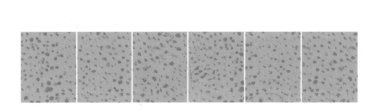
If we cut the granola bar into 6 pieces, each piece is one sixth.

I take $\frac{2}{6}$ of the granola bar.

I take $\frac{3}{6}$ of the granola bar.

2 sixths and 3 sixths make 5 sixths.

$$\frac{2}{6} + \frac{3}{6} = \frac{5}{6}$$

Altogether, they take $\frac{5}{6}$ of the granola bar.

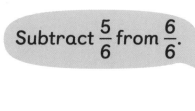
Subtract $\frac{5}{6}$ from $\frac{6}{6}$.

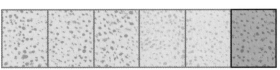

$\frac{1}{6}$ of the granola bar is left.

1 A chocolate bar has 7 equal-sized pieces. Holly takes 2 pieces. Charles takes 2 pieces. What fraction of the chocolate bar is left?

[   ] of the chocolate bar is left.

2 A puzzle is made up of 9 equal parts. Ruby and Elliott complete 2 parts each. Emma completes 1 part.
What fraction of the puzzle hasn't been completed?

[   ] of the puzzle hasn't been completed.

3 A piece of construction paper is cut into 10 equal pieces.
Seven children are each given 1 piece.
What fraction of the construction paper is left?

[   ] of the construction paper is left.

Equivalent Fractions

I take $\frac{1}{4}$ of the cake.

I take $\frac{2}{8}$ of the cake.

Do Jacob and Amira take the same amount of cake?

Example

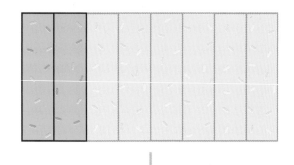

2 eighths is equal to 1 quarter.

$$\frac{2}{8} = \frac{1}{4}$$

÷2

÷2

When 2 parts become 1 part, 8 parts become 4 parts.

$\frac{2}{8}$ is equivalent to $\frac{1}{4}$. They are equivalent fractions.

$\frac{1}{4}$ is the simplest form of $\frac{2}{8}$.

Jacob and Amira take the same amount of cake.

1 Fill in the blanks to complete the equivalent fractions.

(a) $\dfrac{3}{9} = \dfrac{\boxed{}}{3}$

(b) $\dfrac{6}{10} = \dfrac{3}{\boxed{}}$

(c) $\dfrac{8}{12} = \dfrac{\boxed{}}{36}$

2 Give your answers in the simplest form.

(a) Elliott and Hannah had a whole watermelon.

Elliott took $\dfrac{1}{6}$ of the watermelon. Hannah took $\dfrac{3}{6}$ of the watermelon.

How much of the watermelon was left?

$\boxed{} + \boxed{} = \boxed{}$

$\boxed{} - \boxed{} = \boxed{}$

$\boxed{}$ of the watermelon was left.

(b) Ruby bought a dozen doughnuts. She and her friends ate $\dfrac{3}{4}$ of them.

What fraction of the dozen was left?

$\boxed{}$ of the dozen was left.

Comparing Fractions

Starter

Holly ate $\frac{2}{3}$ of a pizza. Emma ate $\frac{3}{5}$ of a pizza. Who ate more?

Example

1

Holly

$\frac{1}{3}$	$\frac{1}{3}$	$\frac{1}{3}$

Emma

$\frac{1}{5}$	$\frac{1}{5}$	$\frac{1}{5}$	$\frac{1}{5}$	$\frac{1}{5}$

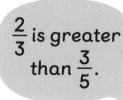

$\frac{2}{3}$ is greater than $\frac{3}{5}$.

$\frac{2}{3}$ is more than $\frac{3}{5}$.

Holly ate more than Emma.

1 Compare $\frac{3}{5}$ and $\frac{3}{4}$.

$\frac{3}{5}$ | | | | |

$\frac{3}{4}$ | | | |

☐ is greater than ☐.

2 Compare $\frac{4}{5}$ and $\frac{4}{7}$.

☐ is less than ☐.

3 Ravi drank $\frac{1}{3}$ l of milk, Charles drank $\frac{2}{5}$ l of milk, and Hannah drank $\frac{3}{8}$ l.

(a) Who drank the most milk? ☐

(b) Who drank the least? ☐

Sharing More Than 1

Starter

Four 1-liter cartons of orange juice are shared equally between 3 pitchers. How much orange juice is in each pitcher?

Example

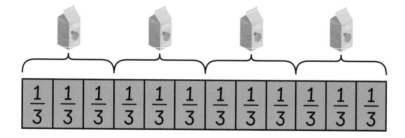

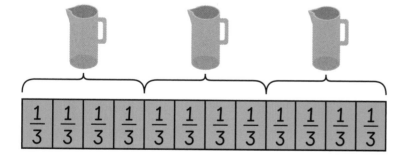

Each pitcher has $\frac{4}{3}$ l of orange juice.

We write 4 thirds as $\frac{4}{3}$.

1 4 children share 5 oranges equally.
How many oranges does each child get?

Each child gets ⬚ oranges.

2 5 children share 4 pies equally.
How much pie does each child get?

Each child gets ⬚ of a pie.

3 6 friends share 7 bars of chocolate equally.
How much chocolate does each friend get?

Each friend gets ⬚ bars of chocolate.

Measuring Time

Starter

Ravi and his mom get on a train at 10:45 a.m. They get off the train at 11:20 a.m.

For how many minutes were they on the train?

Example

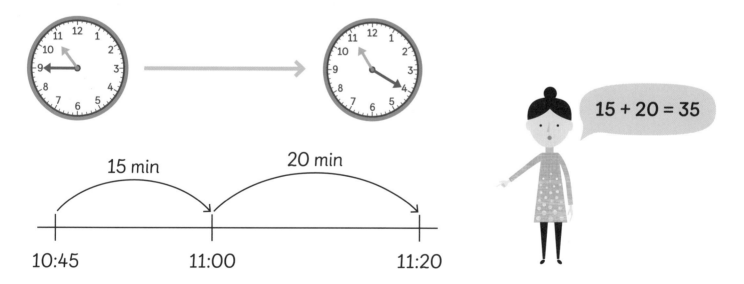

$15 + 20 = 35$

15 min

20 min

10:45   11:00   11:20

Ravi and his mom were on the train for 35 minutes.

1 Solve and fill in the blanks.

The school bell rings at 10:55 a.m. to start recess. It rings again at 11:15 a.m. to end recess. How long is recess?

10:55	11:00	11:15

[ ] + [ ] = [ ]

Recess is [ ] minutes long.

2 Emma started watching a TV show at 6:52 p.m.
She finished watching the show at 7:30 p.m.
How long was the show in minutes?

The show was [ ] minutes long.

3 Charles started reading his book at 7:43 p.m. He read for 45 minutes.
At what time did Charles stop reading his book?

Charles stopped reading his book at [ ] .

Changing Years to Months

Starter

Today is Sam's 8th birthday.
His younger brother is 6 years and 6 months old.
What are their ages in months?

Example

Sam is 8 years old.
There are 12 months in a year.
I can work out how many months old Sam is like this.

1 year = 12 months
2 years = 24 months
4 years = 48 months
8 years = 96 months

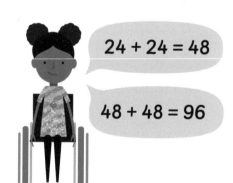

24 + 24 = 48

48 + 48 = 96

We can also just multiply.
$8 \times 12 = 96$

Sam is 96 months old.

Sam's younger brother is 6 years and 6 months old. First we multiply to find how many months there are in 6 years.

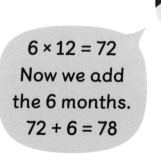

$6 \times 12 = 72$
Now we add the 6 months.
$72 + 6 = 78$

Sam's younger brother is 78 months old.

1 Fill in the blanks.

(a) 5 years = ☐ months

(b) ☐ years = 36 months

(c) 4 years 9 months = ☐ months

(d) ☐ years = 120 months

2 What is your age in months?

☐

I am ☐ months old.

3 Hannah is 18 months older than her cousin.
Her cousin is 88 months old.
How old is Hannah in years and months?

☐

Hannah is ☐ years and ☐ months old.

Capacity and Volume

Starter

Sam's mom used 12 l of paint to paint 4 walls.
She used an equal amount of paint on each of the walls.
How many liters of paint did she use for each wall?

Example

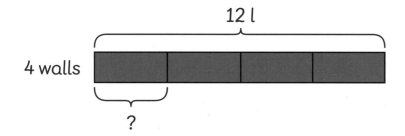

Check.
4 × 3 = 12

$12 \div 4 = 3$

Sam's mom used 3 l of paint for each wall.

1 Elliott uses 21 l of water a week to water his vegetable garden.
He uses the same volume of water each day.
What is the volume of water Elliott uses each day?

$\boxed{} \div \boxed{} = \boxed{}$

Elliott uses $\boxed{}$ of water each day.

2 The volume of juice in a bottle is 3 times the volume of juice in a box.
If the volume of juice in the bottle and the box is 800 ml in total, what is
the volume of juice in the box?

The volume of juice in the box is $\boxed{}$.

3 Oak uses a pitcher to transfer water into her fish tank. She fills and
empties the pitcher into the fish tank 5 times in order to fill it. The fish tank
holds 15 l of water. What is the capacity of the pitcher?

The capacity of the the pitcher is $\boxed{}$.

Estimating Amounts of Money

Starter

Hannah has $30. She rounds the prices of these three items to the nearest $ to estimate the total cost.
Does Hannah have enough money to buy all the items?

$11.40

$7.50

$9.80

Example

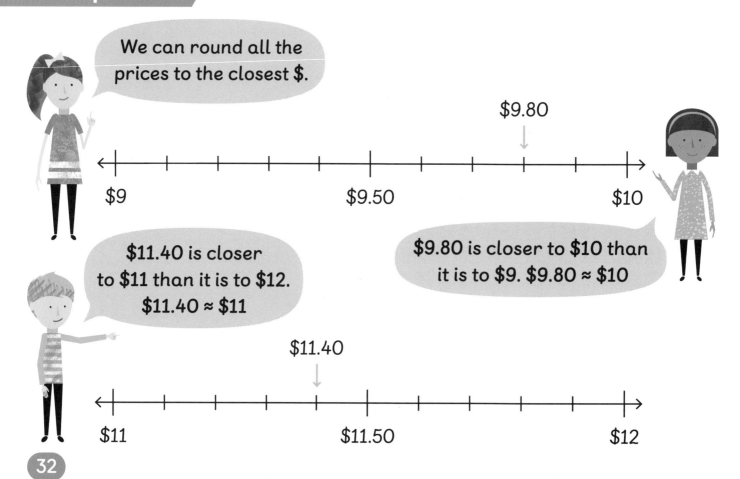

We can round all the prices to the closest $.

$9.80

$9 $9.50 $10

$9.80 is closer to $10 than it is to $9. $9.80 ≈ $10

$11.40 is closer to $11 than it is to $12. $11.40 ≈ $11

$11.40

$11 $11.50 $12

32

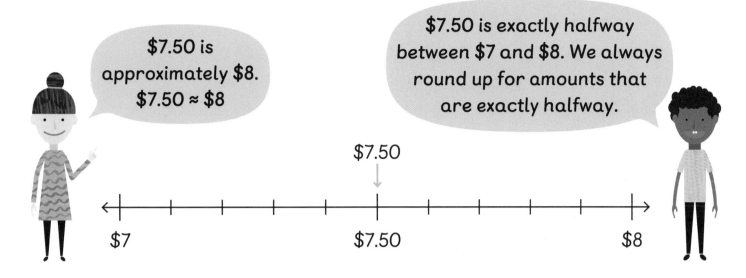

$7.50 is approximately $8.
$7.50 ≈ $8

$7.50 is exactly halfway between $7 and $8. We always round up for amounts that are exactly halfway.

$7.50

$7 $7.50 $8

$10 + $11 + $8 = $29

Hannah has enough money to buy all the items.

Practice

Estimate the total cost of the meal by rounding each item to the nearest $.

1 $3.75 ≈ $ ☐

2 $2.25 ≈ $ ☐

3 $2.50 ≈ $ ☐

Pete's Pasta House

Server : Charlotte
Dine in
Table : 62

Spaghetti Bolognese $3.75
Garlic bread $2.25
Ice cream $2.50

Total Amount

4   The total cost of the meal is about $ ☐.

Writing Amounts of Money

How much money does Holly have in her wallet?

Example

Not all the coins are the same. They have different values.

$1 has the same value as ten 10¢ coins.

10¢ is one tenth of a dollar. We can write 10¢ as $0.10.

 =

$1 has the same value as two 50¢ coins.

 =

50¢ has the same value as five 10¢ coins. We can write it as $0.50.

 =

= $2.00

 = $0.50

 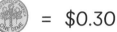 = $0.30

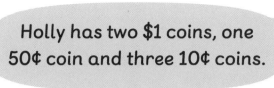
Holly has two $1 coins, one 50¢ coin and three 10¢ coins.

We can add $2.00, $0.50, and $0.30.
$2.00 + $0.50 + $0.30 = $2.80

Holly has $2.80 in her wallet.

Practice

Write the amount of money shown.

1 $ [ ]

2 $ [ ]

3 $ [ ]

4 $ [ ]

Calculating Change

Hannah bought a skateboard and
a helmet using three $20 bills.
How much change did she receive?

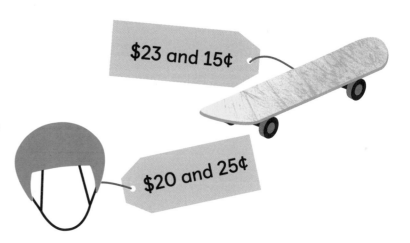

$23 and 15¢

$20 and 25¢

Example

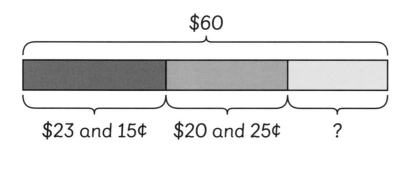

$60

$23 and 15¢ $20 and 25¢   ?

3 × $20 = $60

Add the cents.
15¢ + 25¢ = 40¢

Add the dollars.
$23 + $20 = $43

Hannah paid $43 and 40¢ for the
skateboard and the helmet.

Subtract $43 and
40¢ from $60.

$60 − $43 and 40¢ = $16 and 60¢
Hannah received $16 and 60¢ change.

Use the pictures to answer the questions.

$18 and 35¢

$20 and 10¢

$10 and 20¢

$15 and 65¢

1 Amira bought a cap and a bag with a $50 bill.
How much change did she get?

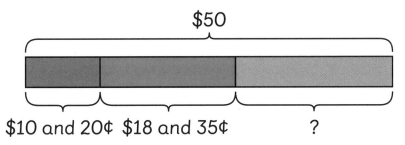

$50

$10 and 20¢ $18 and 35¢   ?

Amira got [   ] change.

2 Sam bought a pair of sunglasses and a pair of shoes. He paid with two
$20 bills. How much change did he get?

Sam got [   ] change.

Calculating Amounts of Money

Starter

The price of a scooter is $124. The price of a bicycle is $240 more than the price of the scooter. The price of a pair of ice skates is $130 less than the bicycle.

What is the price of the bicycle and the ice skates?

Example

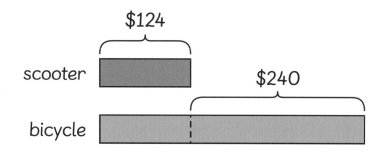

$124

scooter

$240

bicycle

Start by finding the price of the bicycle.

$124 + $240 = $364
The price of the bicycle is $364.

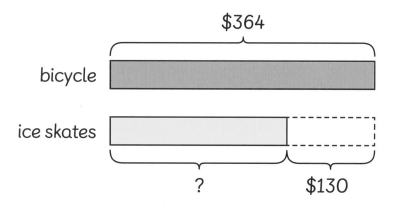

$364

bicycle

ice skates

? $130

Next, find the price of the ice skates.

$364 − $130 = $234
The price of the ice skates is $234.

1 A hoodie is 4 times the price of a shirt. A pair of gloves is half the price of the hoodie.
If the price of the gloves is $12, what are the prices of the shirt and the hoodie?

shirt

hoodie

gloves

$12

The price of the hoodie is [   ].   The price of the shirt is [   ].

2 A plumber spends 3 times as much money on materials than a builder spends. An electrician spends twice as much as the plumber spends.
If the plumber, builder, and electrician spend $160 altogether, how much does each of them spend?

The builder spends [   ].   The plumber spends [   ].

The electrician spends [   ].

Geometry: Perimeter

Starter

Jacob cuts out a rectangle from a larger rectangle.

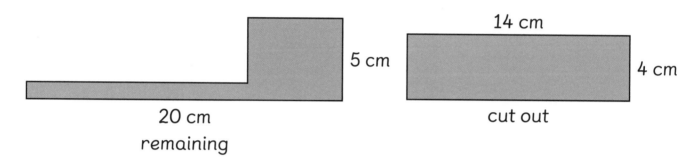

What is the perimeter of the remaining shape?

Example

Start by working out the length of each side of the remaining shape.

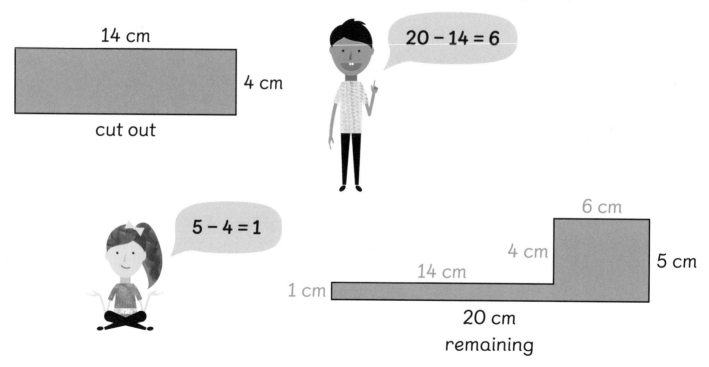

14 cm

4 cm

cut out

20 − 14 = 6

5 − 4 = 1

1 cm

14 cm

4 cm

6 cm

5 cm

20 cm
remaining

Add the lengths of the sides of the remaining shape.
The perimeter of the remaining shape is 50 cm.

1 Oak cuts a piece from a square cake.
Find the perimeter of the remaining shape.

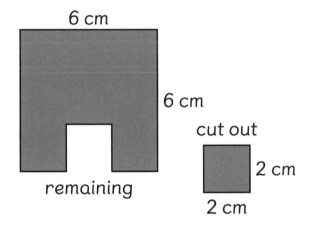

6 cm

6 cm

cut out

2 cm

remaining

2 cm

The perimeter of the remaining shape is [   ] .

2 A carpenter cuts two pieces from a rectangle of wood.
Find the perimeter of the remaining shape.

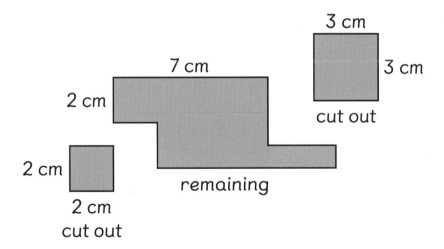

3 cm

7 cm

3 cm

2 cm

cut out

2 cm

2 cm

remaining

2 cm

cut out

The perimeter of the remaining shape is [   ] .

Measuring Area

Starter

Elliott puts his book down on Jacob's drawing.
Is it still possible to find the area of the rectangle that Jacob drew?

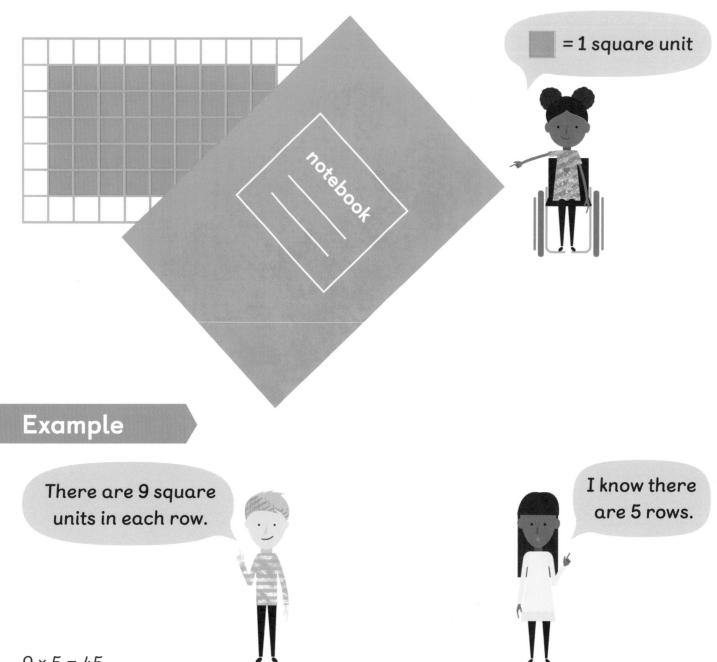

= 1 square unit

Example

There are 9 square
units in each row.

I know there
are 5 rows.

9 × 5 = 45

It is still possible to find the area of the rectangle. It is 45 square units.

Practice

Find the area of each of these rectangles before the corners were cut off.

☐ = 1 square unit

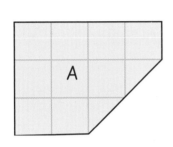

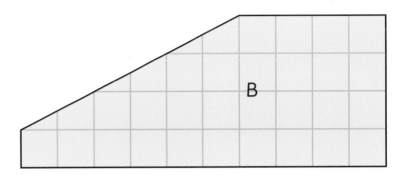

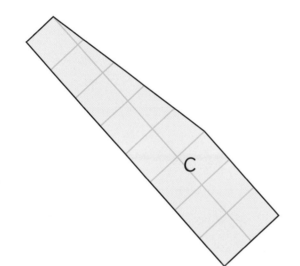

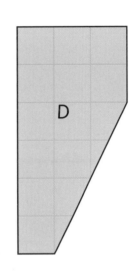

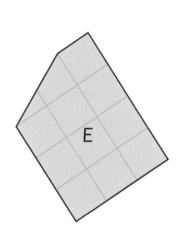

1 Area of A = ☐ square units   **2** Area of B = ☐ square units

3 Area of C = ☐ square units   **4** Area of D = ☐ square units

5 Area of E = ☐ square units

Roman Numerals

Starter

Roman numerals are a number system developed in ancient Rome in which letters represent numbers. This is how the Romans wrote numerals for 1 to 20.

I	= 1	XI	= 11
II	= 2	XII	= 12
III	= 3	XIII	= 13
IV	= 4	XIV	= 14
V	= 5	XV	= 15
VI	= 6	XVI	= 16
VII	= 7	XVII	= 17
VIII	= 8	VIII	= 18
IX	= 9	XIX	= 19
X	= 10	XX	= 20

How can we write greater numbers using Roman numerals?

Example

We use the system for writing numbers 1 to 20 to work out how to write greater numbers.

II = 2	XX = 20
III = 3	XXX = 30

4 is written as 1 less than 5.
IV = 4

40 is written as 10 less than 50.
XL = 40

L is 50 so 60 is written as LX, 70 as LXX and 80 as LXXX.

Writing 10 before 100 makes 90.
XC = 90

C = 100

Practice

1 The chapter numbers in Ravi's book are written in Roman numerals. What do these Roman numerals stand for?

(a)

XIII – The Dark Night

XIII = _____

(b)

XXIV – Here Once More

XXIV = _____

(c)

XLVI – The End is Close

XLVI = _____

2 Write the following numbers using Roman numerals.

(a) 88 = _____

(b) 49 = _____

(c) 44 = _____

(d) 99 = _____

Answers

Page 5   **1 (a)** 874 **(b)** 134 **(c)** 873 **(d)** 137 **2** 134, 137, 873, 874 **3 (a–b)** 963, 936, 693, 639, 396, 369

Page 7   **1 (a)** 2345 + 10 = 2355, 2345 + 9 = 2354 **(b)** 100 + 587 = 687, 99 + 587 = 686 **(c)** 3269 + 500 = 3769, 3269 + 499 = 3768 **(d)** 4231 + 4000 = 8231, 4231 + 3998 = 8229 **2 (a)** 999 + 2999 = 3998 **(b)** 999 + 3001 = 4000 **(c)** 5997 + 998 = 6995 **(d)** 3998 + 5998 = 9996

Page 9   **1 (a)** 43 − 19 = 24 **(b)** 101 − 99 = 2 **(c)** 803 − 198 = 605 **(d)** 1000 − 326 = 674 **(e)** 5000 − 1674 = 3326 **(f)** 9008 − 99 = 8909 **2 (a)** 1001 − 999 = 2 **(b)** 1001 − 199 = 802 **(c)** 700 − 675 = 25 **(d)** 1700 − 1575 = 125

Page 11   **1** He bakes 525 brown dinner rolls. **2** He bakes 921 dinner rolls altogether. **3** Altogether, 223 dinner rolls are left over.

Page 13   **1** 42 × 7 = 294. There are 294 rulers in the 7 classrooms altogether. **2** 24 × 9 = 216. The children buy 216 stickers altogether.

Page 14   **1** 70 ÷ 5 = 14. Each child gets 14 tennis balls.

Page 15   **2** 52 ÷ 4 = 13. They make 13 piles of books. **3** 3 × 28 = 84, 84 ÷ 6 = 14. The children plant 14 rows of seeds altogether.

Page 16   **1** Lulu has 30 books.

Page 17   **2** Bus A takes 54 children. Bus B takes 18 children. Bus C takes 28 children. **3** There are 168 crayons altogether.

Page 19   **1** $\frac{3}{7}$ of the chocolate bar is left. **2** $\frac{4}{9}$ of the puzzle hasn't been completed. **3** $\frac{3}{10}$ of the construction paper is left.